KT-116-361

Contents

Introduction

A plane flies overhead as your bus arrives at the station. You use a cash card to withdraw money at the station, buy your ticket and then board the train bound for the Channel Tunnel. Some of the other passengers are using mobile phones; others work away at their laptop computers. Within a few hours you will be standing beneath the Eiffel Tower.

Today, none of the details listed above – the bus, train, cashpoint, mobile phone or personal computer – would be anything out of the ordinary. Yet a century or two ago they would have been unheard of, along with the idea of getting to Paris in a few hours. All of those modern-day items can trace their origins to an inventive and world-changing period known as the Industrial Revolution. The term 'revolution' is a good one because, like political revolutions, the Industrial Revolution replaced an old way of life with something very new and different. Before the Industrial Revolution, people had none of these modern products and, just as importantly, they had no way of making them.

What was the Industrial Revolution?

The Industrial Revolution was a time of invention and new developments. It began in England in the eighteenth century as people began to look for new ways to produce things on a greater scale. Many of the inventions developed were machines that could do the work of many people. The machines themselves, along with some of the goods they produced, were made of **durable** materials such as iron and steel. To power these machines, inventors used new sources of energy: first water power, then steam and coal and, more recently, oil-based fuels and electricity.

Over the space of just a few decades, individual producers (of crops, **textiles**, iron and other products) were replaced by modern farms and factories that could supply growing towns and cities more easily. Goods could be grown or produced at much lower costs. These costs dropped even further because trains, trucks and other new types of transport could ship large amounts of goods cheaply. By the twentieth century many products for sale were made in factories.

In the nineteenth century, industrial towns like this quickly grew up, especially in the north of England. Factory buildings towered over the terraces of brick houses where workers lived.

Widespread changes

The wide-ranging change produced by the Industrial Revolution would certainly bring many comforts and benefits for ordinary people. The modern items listed on the previous page are recent examples, but we can also thank the Industrial Revolution for the electric light, the telephone, the aeroplane and the **technology** that can send astronauts into space. The same revolution, however, brought dull working conditions, health hazards and pollution on a wide scale. The Industrial Revolution is continuing today with each new development in industry and technology. Will future generations be able to enjoy the benefits of the revolution without suffering such side effects?

The method of producing goods quickly and cheaply in factories started with the Industrial Revolution. Modern goods today, such as stereos and televisions, are produced in much the same way.

5

How do we know?

By studying history, we can learn about the events of the past. If, for example, we need to find out about the original Olympic Games or the French Revolution, we can find many books and articles about these subjects. They can tell us when and how these events took place, as well as who were the leading characters. They often explain why things have happened, by giving the background to the events, and also describe how the events themselves changed the course of history.

Although these works are helpful and informative, they are often written many years (sometimes many centuries) after the events they describe. Like any story that is told, some changes can creep into the accounts. Perhaps the historian did not like sport, or French people, or **revolutionaries** generally. That attitude of mind can affect how the story gets told, because the historian wants to present the facts as he or she wanted them to occur. The historian might leave out some of the facts that do not fit into this view of the world. Such a personal opinion is called **bias**, and it makes some historical accounts unreliable.

Of course, a historian might have no personal opinion on the matter, but he or she still may use other accounts that were written long after the events. Such accounts are called **secondary sources**, because the historian arrives at them second-hand. Here again we must take care in deciding on the truth. The second historian, basing his or her history on earlier retellings, might be repeating the bias or even mistakes of the previous accounts. Each retelling increases the risk of bias and inaccuracy.

In 2001 US President Bush and Russian President Putin meet to discuss the war in Afghanistan. They tell newspaper reporters about their discussions. Historians of the future may read the newspapers to help them understand world events in the early 21st century.

Getting to the source

This book aims to use **primary sources** to tell the story of the Industrial Revolution. Secondary sources can obviously give us the broad picture of how this important historical period changed the way we work and live. But the primary sources capture the 'feel' of the times, keeping pace with the fast-moving changes that amazed many people and horrified others. These accounts – diary entries, government reports, memoirs and household records – give a human face to a time when people saw so much of their lives changing.

> ### TO
> # Journeymen Spinners
> ### Wanted Immediately,
> From Eighty to One Hundred
> # MULE SPINNERS,
> For a New Mill and other Mills, in Great Bolton, which New Mill is complete with new Machinery now ready gaited, and will commence running on Monday Morning next, adjoining to which Mills are a Number of Cottages, for the convenience and accommodation of Spinners: liberal Wages will be given and constant employ.
> For further particulars apply to Messrs. ORMROD and HARDCASTLE, of Bolton aforesaid, Cotton Spinners.

An advertisement from 1816 for workers for a new cotton mill in the north of England. Details in advertisements like this help us build up a picture of the Industrial Revolution.

Making our minds up

Not every primary source is truly without bias and that is true of some of the sources you will find in this book. The Industrial Revolution was a time of bold invention; and many of the inventors faced criticism and hardship before their work was recognised. You can sense the pride, for example, in Marconi's account of his first wireless message (see pages 44–45) or Orville Wright's description of his first flight (see pages 46–47). Other documents served to alert the public about dangers or to make a political point. The parliamentary report into child labour (see pages 16–17) and George Sims's description of a poor London family (see pages 42–43) are good examples. Many of the other accounts are simple descriptions of developments in a fast-changing world. Together they help us get a fuller idea of life in that fascinating period of world history.

Life before the Industrial Revolution

In order to understand the importance of the Industrial Revolution, we need to know what life was like before it. In our modern era, we often speak of the 'pace of change'. The latest computer can seem outdated or under-powered after only a year; a 30-year-old television looks like an antique. Things were not always like that.

If we look at life in the year 1700 (roughly the beginning of the Industrial Revolution), many things had remained unchanged for centuries. Life was mainly based on farming, with families producing enough goods for their own needs. Craftworkers also worked on a local level, making and mending things for their neighbours with little contact with the world beyond their own village. The slow pace of life was hardly different from that of the Middle Ages. Water mills, windmills and horses or oxen provided the only extra power, and most work was still done by hand. Few people realized that all this was set to change.

Before the Industrial Revolution farming was the main activity, and power was provided by animals, such as oxen or horses. Farmers often worked from sunrise to sunset, and most people spent their whole lives in the same village where they were born.

Benjamin Franklin's experience

In the time before the Industrial Revolution boys began working at an early age, learning crafts or trades. The great American statesman Benjamin Franklin (1706–90) here describes how his father tried to find a trade suitable for his young son.

At ten years old I was taken home to assist my father in his business, which was that of a tallow-chandler and soap-boiler; a business he was not bred to, but had assumed on his arrival in New England, and on finding his dying trade would not maintain his family, being in little request. Accordingly, I was employed in cutting wick for the candles, filling the dipping mold and the molds for cast candles, attending the shop, going on errands, etc.

I continued thus employed in my father's business for two years, that is, till I was twelve years old; and my brother John, who was bred to that business, having left my father, married, and set up for himself at Rhode Island, there was all appearance that I was destined to supply his place, and become a tallow-chandler. But my dislike to the trade continuing, my father tried to find me another craft. He therefore sometimes took me to walk with him, and see **joiners**, bricklayers, **turners**, brass workers, etc, at their work, that he might observe my inclination, and endeavor to fix it on some trade or other on land.

Benjamin Franklin eventually became a printer and newspaper proprietor. He also helped draft America's Declaration of Independence.

The new Iron Age

Iron was an important material in the Industrial Revolution. It was strong and **durable**, and could be put to all sorts of uses in building and manufacturing. People had known how to make iron (by heating iron **ore** to produce pure iron) for thousands of years, but it had never been produced in large quantities. However, by the eighteenth century there was a huge demand for iron and many iron **smelters** served the needs of England alone.

Furnaces had to be kept hot all the time to produce these large quantities of iron. This meant using huge amounts of timber, which could be turned into **charcoal**. The English iron worker and inventor Abraham Darby developed a way of using **coke**, rather than wood, to smelt iron in 1709. The new process promised to be cheaper and more efficient than burning wood and charcoal. Coke came from coal, and Britain was only just beginning to use its coal reserves. In the meantime, vast areas of English forests and woodlands were cleared to feed the iron-making furnaces.

The description by Daniel Defoe on the opposite page is one of the first accounts of what we now term the Industrial Revolution. Defoe knew the landscape of southern England well and he could see how the widespread cutting down of trees was changing the environment. We can read his account as a warning about **deforestation**. He knew that it would be hard – if not impossible – to replace these trees. Similarly, we use fuels such as oil and gas to supply our energy needs, but like the trees in Defoe's England, these natural resources are precious and vital to our way of life. However, they too are irreplaceable, and one day they will also run out. Defoe appears to have been very aware of the negative effects of the march of progress.

Daniel Defoe's description
Daniel Defoe, author of *Robinson Crusoe*, wrote widely on subjects closer to home. In this passage from 1726 he describes the conditions in the Weald, a wooded part of the county of Kent, in southern England. The Weald was a centre of the iron industry because of all its timber.

Once the Industrial Revolution started, many men found jobs in factories or ironworks like this one. Iron was used to make machines and tools, and to build bridges and ships.

All this part of the country is agreeably pleasant, wholesome and fruitful, I mean quite from Guildford to this place [Westerham, Kent], and is accordingly overspread with good towns, gentlemen's houses, populous villages and the lands well cultivated; but all on the right hand, that is to say, south, is exceedingly grown with timber, has abundance of waste, and wild grounds and forests and woods, at which they cast great quantities of iron cauldrons, chimney-backs, furnaces and all such necessary things of iron; besides iron cannon, and cannon ball etc. in an infinite quantity, and which turn to very great account; tho' at the same time the works are prodigiously expensive, and the quantity of wood they consume is exceeding great, which keeps up that complaint that I mentioned before; that timber would grow scarce and consequently dear, from the great quantity consumed in the iron-works in Sussex.

King Cotton

The southern half of the United States has a warm, humid climate that is ideal for growing one of the **raw materials** used for clothing – cotton. Southern farmers had been growing cotton since the seventeenth century, on huge farms called plantations. Slaves were shipped in from Africa to work on the cotton plantations, but the farmers could not find a way of **processing** large amounts of the cotton quickly. The cotton producers simply could not keep pace with the growing demand.

The breakthrough came in 1793, when Eli Whitney developed his cotton gin – a device to remove the seeds from raw cotton. The invention changed farming in America almost overnight. It also made cotton the basis of the American South's **economy**. Cotton plantations – and their owners – began making much more money, and cotton became one of the most important **exports** of the United States. Within a decade of Whitney's invention, 'King Cotton' ruled nearly half of the country.

Eli Whitney invented a machine for separating the seeds from the raw cotton fibres. His invention helped make the United States the world's leading cotton producer.

Thomas Jefferson's letter
Thomas Jefferson, who became the third president of the United States in 1801, was from Virginia and knew how important cotton was to the South. He was keen to try out new inventions, and recognized the value of the cotton gin, as this letter to Eli Whitney proves.

Germantown, Nov. 16. 1793.

Sir,-Your favor of Oct. 15. inclosing a drawing of your cotton gin, was received on the 6th inst. The only requisite of the law now uncomplied with is the forwarding a model, which being received your patent may be made out & delivered to your order immediately.

As the state of Virginia, where I live, carries on household manufactures of cotton to a great extent, as I also do myself, and one of our great embarrassments is the clearing of the cotton of the seed, I feel a considerable interest in the success of your invention, for family use. Permit me therefore to ask information from you on these points. Has the machine been thoroughly tried in the ginning of cotton, or is it as yet but a machine of theory?

Slaves operate the cotton gin. With the use of this new invention plantation owners could keep up with the huge demand for cotton.

What quantity of cotton has it cleaned on an average of several days, & worked by hand, & by how many hands? What will be the cost of one of them made to be worked by hand? Favorable answers to these questions would induce me to engage one of them to be forwarded to Richmond for me. Wishing to hear from you on the subject I am &c.

P.S. Is this the machine advertised the last year by Pearce at the Patterson manufactory?

Weaving the future

While the American South entered a new age of cotton production (allowing it to send vast quantities abroad), Great Britain found ways of mass-producing high-quality **textiles**. It soon became the most important market for American cotton, while home-produced wool was also an important **raw material** for the growing British textile industry.

By the mid-1700s textiles had become an important part of Britain's industrial development. The industry benefited from a number of inventions, which allowed single machines to do the same amount of work that once needed many individuals. One of these inventions was James Hargreaves' spinning jenny, developed in 1764. The spinning jenny speeded up weaving the **warp** in the production of cloth by allowing a single person to spin many separate yarns at the same time. Other inventions improved and developed this process, so that by the end of the eighteenth century the textile industry was transformed. The workers, who had once been individual craftspeople, now became machine operators. Other industries would soon follow this example.

Women and young girls often worked the machinery in cotton factories. The new machines took the place of individual weavers and speeded up the process of making cloth.

A 1794 description of a weaving factory

This extract is taken from 'Observations on the Loss of Woollen Spinning', a 1794 account of the sweeping changes taking place in English industry. Many of the workers in the weaving 'factory' were young girls. Child labour would become an important feature of the Industrial Revolution.

I then walked to the Machines, and with some difficulty gained admittance: there I saw both the Combing Machine and Spinning Jenny. The Combing Machine was put in motion by a Wheel turned by four men, but which I am sure could be turned either by water or steam. The frames were supplied by a child with Wool, and as the wheel turned, flakes of ready combed Wool dropped off a cylinder into a trough, these were taken up by a girl of about fourteen years old, who placed them on the Spinning Jenny, which has a number of horizontal beams of wood, on each of which may be fifty **bobbins**. One such girl sets these bobbins all in motion by turning a wheel at the end of the beam, a wire then catches up a flake of Wool, spins it, and gathers it upon each bobbin. The girl again turns the wheel, and another fifty flakes are taken up and Spun. This is done every minute without intermission, so that probably one girl turning that wheel, may do the work of One Hundred Hand Wheels at the least. About twenty of these sets of bobbins, were, I judge, at work in one room. Most of these [factories] are many stories high, and the rooms much larger than this I was in.

Child labour

One of the most disturbing aspects of the Industrial Revolution was the number of children who were forced to work long hours in factories. These workers, some as young as five years old, usually earned tiny wages and had to put up with dirty, dangerous conditions. Many suffered broken limbs or severe burns because of the machinery. The issue of child labour became more and more important as new factories opened across Britain. People began to question whether the growing national wealth was actually based on cruelty against defenceless workers. Children working in factories and mills had no way of publicizing their conditions, as they would be dismissed if they tried.

A group of people, known as social **reformers**, took up the cause of child labour in the 1830s. In 1832 Michael Sadler headed a parliamentary committee that studied conditions in **textile** factories. The stories of harsh conditions prompted the committee to push for new laws to protect these young workers. The result was the Act of 1833, which limited hours of employment for women and children in textile work.

Young children were used as workers in the new mills and factories. They were often overworked and cruelly treated.

Committee's interview with Peter Smart

Michael Sadler's committee interviewed many young workers to learn about conditions in factories. This extract shows how the questions (usually from Sadler himself) were designed to uncover as much as possible.

Peter Smart, called in, and questioned.

MS You say you were locked up night and day?
PS —Yes.
MS Do the children ever attempt to run away?
PS —Very often.
MS Were they pursued and brought back again?
PS —Yes, the overseer pursued them, and brought them back.
MS Did you ever attempt to run away?
PS —Yes, I ran away twice.
MS And you were brought back?
PS —Yes; and I was sent up to the master's loft, and thrashed with a whip for running away.
MS Were you **bound** to this man?
PS —Yes, for six years.
MS By whom were you bound?
PS —My mother got 15s. for the six years.
MS Do you know whether the children were, in point of fact, compelled to stop during the whole time for which they were engaged?
PS —Yes, they were.
MS By law?
PS —I cannot say by law; but they were compelled by the master; I never saw any law used there but the law of their own hands.
MS To what mill did you next go?
PS —To Mr. Webster's, at Battus Den, within eleven miles of Dundee.
MS In what situation did you act there?
PS —I acted as overseer.
MS At 17 years of age?
PS —Yes
MS How long have you worked per day in order to produce the quantity your master required?
PS —I have worked nineteen hours.
MS To what time have you worked?
PS —I have seen the mill going till it was past 12 o'clock on the Saturday night.
MS So that the mill was still working on the Sabbath morning?
PS —Yes.

Violent reaction

Great Britain led the way in the Industrial Revolution and by the early nineteenth century there were many factories, especially in the north of England and the Midlands. Many workers became worried by the spread of these factories, as they feared that the new machines would leave them without work. Some workers decided to take action, meeting secretly to plan acts of **sabotage**.

In 1811, factory owners in Nottingham began receiving threatening letters signed by 'General Ned Ludd and the Army of **Redressers**'. There was no such person as Ludd, but the factory owners knew that the messages reflected the feelings of real workers. The letters protested at wage reductions and the use of **unapprenticed** workmen. The secret group, soon nicknamed 'Luddites', then broke into factories at night to destroy the new machinery. Luddite protests spread to Yorkshire, Lancashire, Leicestershire and Derbyshire. Factory owners became fearful, and the Government offered fifty pounds reward for help in arresting the culprits. By 1815 the movement had been stopped, but factory owners – and the public – realized that many felt threatened by the new factories and machinery. Other countries also experienced such violent reactions, as new labour practices took hold.

Luddites protested against the new industries by breaking into factories and smashing the new machinery. They feared that the machines would leave them without work.

Archibald Prentice's account

Archibald Prentice wrote about the Luddite disturbances in April 1812 in his book *Historical Sketches and Personal Recollections of Manchester*. His account captures the feeling of a group of people whose world was turning upside down. Old ways of working were disappearing, and being replaced with dreary working conditions and dangerous machinery.

On Saturday, the 18th April, a large group of people, chiefly women, assembled at the potato market, Shude Hill, where the sellers were asking 14s. and 15s. per load (252 lbs.) for potatoes. Some of the women began forcibly to take possession of the articles; but police and soldiers intervened, to fix a sort of maximum, for eight shillings per load, at which they were sold in small portions. On 27th April a riotous assembly took place at Middleton. The weaving factory of Mr. Burton and Sons had been previously threatened because they used steam power for their weaving. The factory was protected by soldiers, so strongly as to be able to withstand to their assault; they then flew to the house of Mr. Emanuel Burton, where they took revenge by setting it on fire. On Friday, the 24th April, a large body of weavers and mechanics began to assemble about midday, intending to detroy the power-looms, together with the whole factory, at Westhoughton. The military rode at full speed to Westhoughton where they found that the premises were entirely destroyed and not an individual could be seen who might have acted a part in this truly dreadful outrage.

Coal mining

One of the most important changes brought about by the Industrial Revolution was the way in which power was obtained. Some of the earliest factories simply used water power – the force of flowing water was enough to power mill wheels. Others used wind power or even manpower – workers turning a mill wheel by hand. New industries required even more power than these sources could supply. This extra power was provided by coal, which was burned in large quantities in blast-furnaces, forges and foundries. It was also a main fuel for the steam engines used in the **textile** and other industries.

Britain had large reserves of coal and the increased demand led to mines being dug deeper and deeper. These deep mines presented safety problems. One obvious risk was that the mines themselves might collapse, trapping and killing dozens of miners. Fire and explosions were other grave dangers. Gases and coal dust – both highly **inflammable** – could collect in the deep mine shafts. If they came into contact with a miner's candle or a spark caused by a metal tool, they could trigger a terrible explosion and collapse the mine.

After one explosion in a mine killed 92 men and boys, Sir Humphrey Davy designed the first miners' safety lamp. The lamp's wire mesh screened the flame and prevented sparks escaping.

A newspaper article
Mining disasters became common in the nineteenth century. This is a local newspaper account of an explosion in a **colliery** in Wallsend, in 1821.

WALLSEND EXPLOSION

October 23, - a dreadful explosion took place in Wallsend colliery, by which fifty-two men lost their lives. The explosion shook the ground like an earthquake, and made the furniture dance in the surrounding houses. This alarming the neighbourhood, the friends and relatives hurried to the spot, when a heart-rending scene of distress ensued. The greatest exertions were instantly made by Mr. Buddle, the viewer, who, as soon as it was practicable, descended with his assistants, when a most melancholy scene presented itself. At the time of the explosion there were fifty-six men in the pit, of which number only four survived. The bodies of the deceased were most dreadfully scorched, and many of them most strangely distorted. Forty-six of the bodies were buried in one grave; some of the remainder were buried at the Ballasthills, and some at Wallsend old church, amidst sorrowing spectators.

An underground explosion was a constant fear for miners working deep below the surface of the earth. If the men were not killed by the explosion, the collapsing mine would crush them.

An age of invention

The Industrial Revolution was truly an age of invention, when scientific and technical discoveries were made that affect all our lives today. Amazingly, plans for the first computer were completed nearly 200 years ago by an English inventor, Charles Babbage. Born in 1791, Babbage grew up in an age when the British government paid inventors for useful new machines.

In the early 1820s Babbage began work on a Difference Engine, a machine to solve simple maths problems. This machine (which Babbage also called a Calculating Machine) was a basic computer. Many fellow scientists refused to believe that such a machine would work. Babbage started to build his Difference Engine, but was unable to complete it because of a lack of funding. In 1991, British scientists followed Babbage's detailed plans and built a Difference Engine. The machine worked perfectly, working out detailed calculations and proving that Babbage's design would have been successful.

Charles Babbage's Difference Engine was designed to calculate numbers. The Board of Longitude offered large sums for inventions that would make Britain an even stronger seafaring nation.

Charles Babbage's diary
These extracts from Babbage's diaries come from the time when he was designing his Difference Engine. We can sense his frustration that other scientists – and the Government – failed to recognize its potential.

May 10th [1822]

My calculating machine is nearly finished. Of those who I have made acquainted with the principles many think too little of it, of those ignorant of them the greater part think far too much.

Monday June 8th [1822]

Maule and Peacock called and examined the Engine, admired it considerably. P candidly confessed that since Herschel first told him of it he had considered the subject and thought it impossible. Maule appeared to take considerable interest in its success but rather doubted it. Dr. Wollaston appointed to meet me at my house in an hour to see the engine. I explained all its parts, and he then worked it and after about an hour and a half the result of his opinion was expressed in these words. 'All this is very pretty but I do not see how it can be rendered productive.'

Thursday 11th June 1822

This morning Davies Gilbert examined the machine and advised that it should be brought before the Board of Longitude. I observed that from what I knew of the Board I did not think it had power or will to do any thing. With respect to the government he observed that they were perfectly unacquainted with the nature of the thing and that the only chance was that Mr Peel [Sir Robert Peel, the Home Secretary] might take it up. He remarked that Dr Young [of the Board] disliked every thing that did not originate with himself.

This small part of Babbage's Difference Engine was completed in 1832. It is the first known automatic calculator.

Canal mania

Factory owners were eager to get their goods to towns and cities quickly and cheaply. They also needed to get **raw materials**, such as cotton, iron **ore** and coal to their factories. The main obstacle was the poor quality of roads and the small loads that packhorses could carry.

The solution seemed to be water transport. After all, ships had been carrying heavy loads – even across oceans – for centuries. British engineers began exploring how a network of canals could link the country's major rivers. Large, flat-bottomed boats would then be able to transport big quantities of goods over great distances. The greater loads would, in turn, reduce the cost of shipment. The initial stretch of Britain's first important canal, the Bridgewater Canal, was completed in 1761. It linked the mines in Worsley with Manchester, where the coal helped power many new factories. Over the next few decades a wide-ranging network of canals was built all across Britain, linking the main industrial centres with major towns and ports. During this period the rush to build canals became known as 'canal **mania**'.

The Bridgewater Canal was Britain's first important canal.
Aqueducts were built so canals could cross rivers.

An account of canal mania

Canals were operated as businesses, raising money by selling **shares** to the public. Share-owners would then be able to have a share of the profits once the canal was operating. This account, from Bristol, gives an idea of what 'canal mania' was like at its height.

On the 20th of November 1792 a meeting to promote the construction of a canal from Bristol to Gloucester was held in the [Bristol] Guildhall, when the scheme was enthusiastically supported by influential persons, and a very large sum was **subscribed** by those present, who struggled violently with each other in their rush to the subscription book. A few days later, a Somerset paper announced that a meeting would be held at Wells to promote a canal from Bristol to Taunton. The design had been formed in this city [Bristol] but the promoters strove to keep it a secret, and bought up all the newspapers containing the advertisement. The news nevertheless leaked out in the evening before the intended gathering, and a host of **speculators** set off to secure shares in the undertaking, some arriving only to find that the subscription list was full. The third meeting was at Devizes, on the 12th of December. Only a day's notice was given of this movement, which was to promote a canal from Bristol to Southampton and London but the news rapidly spread and thousands of intending subscribers rushed to the little town. The 'race to Devizes' on the part of Bristolians who had hired or bought up at absurd prices all the old carriages that could be found, and plunged along the miry roads through a long wintry night, was full of many comic incidents.

Full steam ahead

Since the time of the ancient Greeks, more than 2000 years ago, scientists had noted that air expands when it contains water that has been heated into steam. By the eighteenth century, scientists had worked out how to put this steam to work. In 1705, English engineer Thomas Newcomen built the first commercially successful steam engine. It marked the first important source of power other than wind and water. Other engineers improved on the steam engine and in 1775 James Watt designed an engine that could be used in all sorts of ways. Watt engines began powering mills and other factories, and people wondered whether steam power might also improve sea transport.

One idea was to produce a steam-powered vessel that, unlike sailing ships, would not need to rely on the wind. Several inventors came up with plans, but the first practical steamboat was developed in the United States. In 1807, Robert Fulton's Clermont travelled from New York City to Albany, New York, in about a quarter of the time it would take a sailing vessel.

Fulton's steamboat was propelled by two large paddle wheels. The engine itself burned coal, to heat the water into steam.

Robert Fulton's letter

Fulton was mocked while he built his boat, and some people called it 'Fulton's **Folly**'. He proved them wrong on 17 August 1807, describing the events in a letter to his friend Joel Barlow.

My steamboat voyage to Albany and back has turned out rather more favourably than I had calculated. The distance from New York to Albany is one hundred and fifty miles. I ran it up in thirty-two hours and down in thirty. I had a light breeze against me the whole way both going and coming and the voyage has been performed wholly by the power of the steam-engine. I overtook many sloops and schooners beating to windward and parted with them as if they had been at anchor. The power of propelling boats by steam is now fully proved. The morning I left New York, there were not perhaps thirty persons in the city who believed that the boat would ever move one mile an hour, or be of the least utility, and while we were putting off from the wharf, which was crowded with spectators, I heard a number of sarcastic remarks.

American inventor Robert Fulton transformed water transport with the first successful steamboat. From now on ships need not depend just on wind for power.

Having employed much time, money, and zeal in accomplishing this work, it gives me, as it will you, great pleasure to see it fully answer my expectations. It will give a cheap and quick conveyance to the merchants on the Mississippi, Missouri, and other great rivers which are now laying open their treasures to the enterprise of our countrymen; and although the prospect of personal **emolument** has been some inducement to me, yet I feel infinitely more pleasure in reflecting on the immense advantages that my country will draw from the invention.

The dawn of the Railway Age

Steam, produced by the energy provided by coal, had been the power behind much of the Industrial Revolution. By the nineteenth century nearly every manufactured good in Britain and in some other countries was produced on steam-powered machines. Now many people had the idea of using steam to transport goods – and people – over long distances. Robert Fulton's success with his steamboat (see pages 26–27) gave engineers hope that something similar could be achieved on land.

The answer was the railway. Britain's first regular commercial rail service, linking the northern industrial towns of Stockton and Darlington, opened in 1825. The Liverpool & Manchester Railway opened on 15 September 1830. That same year saw a famous contest in America: inventor Peter Cooper staged a race between his 'Tom Thumb' locomotive and a horse. The horse won because of mechanical problems with the locomotive, but an astonished public saw the power of this new form of transport. The railway offered a means of travel and of shipping goods that would make existing forms of transport seem slow. For Americans the railway meant new opportunities, such as opening up the West to settlement and trade.

On 15 September 1830 the Liverpool & Manchester Railway opened. A network of railways soon criss-crossed the whole of Britain.

Peter Cooper's description of locomotive carriages

Peter Cooper's development of the 'Tom Thumb' locomotive was the first step towards America's westward progress along rail lines. By 1832 Cooper and his Baltimore & Ohio Railroad Company had laid 137 miles of rail track – the longest stretch in the world at the time. They also had to publicize their new form of transport, as this newspaper extract from 1830 shows.

The body of the carriage will contain twelve persons, and the outside seats at either end will receive six, including the driver. On the top of the carriage is placed a double sofa, running length wise, which will accommodate twelve more. A wire netting rises from two sides of the carriage to a height which renders the top seats perfectly secure. The whole is surmounted by an iron framework, with an awning to protect from sun or rain. The carriage, which is named the Ohio, is very handsomely finished.

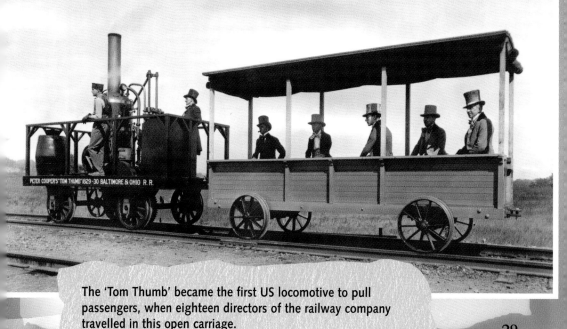

The 'Tom Thumb' became the first US locomotive to pull passengers, when eighteen directors of the railway company travelled in this open carriage.

Capturing an image

For centuries artists had tried to produce accurate pictures of the world around them. The results always depended on their abilities – to paint well, sculpt accurately and generally reproduce what they saw around them. Some inventions, designed to help artists, were developed in the seventeenth century, when scientists were beginning to understand lenses and the properties of light. Both the **camera obscura** and **camera lucida** used lenses to project an image on to a flat surface which the artist could then trace.

The Industrial Revolution also brought changes to the way images were made. The art of photography was pioneered in 1834 by William Fox Talbot of Wiltshire, who produced the first photographs ever seen. He used the same basic technique that is common today: a piece of film is exposed to light to produce a negative image. A series of chemical processes turns this negative image into a positive one, a photograph. Photography captured the public imagination, and Fox Talbot and other early photographers became famous. The process has since provided us not only with enjoyable keepsakes, but with **documentary** evidence of great events.

The photographic process invented by Fox Talbot meant any number of prints could be made from the same negative. This is his photograph of Clare College, Cambridge taken in 1843.

Fox Talbot's account

Fox Talbot would have liked to have been an artist, but he was never satisfied with his painting skills. He turned to photography almost by accident, as he describes in this passage.

In October, 1833, I was amusing myself on the lovely shores of the Lake of Como in Italy, taking sketches with a Camera Lucida, or rather, I should say, attempting to make them; but with the smallest possible amount of success. After various fruitless attempts I laid aside the instrument and came to the conclusion that its use required a previous knowledge of drawing which unfortunately I did not possess.

I then thought of trying again a method which I had tried many years before. This method was to take a Camera Obscura and to throw the image of the objects on a piece of paper in its focus – fairy pictures, creations of a moment, and destined as rapidly to fade away. It was during these thoughts that the idea occurred to me how charming it would be if it were possible to cause these natural images to imprint themselves durably and remain fixed on the paper!

William Fox Talbot's artistic experiments helped to introduce the age of photography. He went on to take thousands of photographs.

Messages in the wires

The first instruments for sending electrical messages along wires (telegraph messages) were invented in the United States by Samuel F. B. Morse in 1837 and in Great Britain the same year by Sir Charles Wheatstone and Sir William F. Cooke. This was a genuine breakthrough in communications, since it meant that people could send and receive messages across huge distances in an instant. Morse soon gained the advantage over his rivals when he developed a simple code (now known as Morse code) in which electric pulses passing over a single wire would represent different letters.

In 1843 the US Congress released $30,000 for Morse to build a telegraph line between Washington, DC, and Baltimore, Maryland. The following year Morse completed his preparations and sent the world's first telegraph message, or telegram. The age of instant communications had begun.

Samuel Morse's transmitter sent the first telegram in 1844. His system of Morse code meant people could communicate over vast distances.

An eyewitness account

Harper's Magazine ran an article (based on eyewitness accounts from the participants) on Morse's great achievement in 1844. The 'bill' refers to the $30,000 that the US Congress approved to enable Morse to build the Washington–Baltimore telegraph line.

By the month of May, 1844, the whole line was laid, and magnets and recording instruments were attached to the ends of the wires at Mount Clare Depot, Baltimore, and at the Supreme Court Chamber, in the Capitol at Washington. When the circuit was complete, and the signal at the one end of the line was responded to by the operator at the other, Mr. Morse sent a messenger to Miss Ellsworth to inform her that the telegraph awaited her message. She speedily responded to this, and sent for transmission the following message, which was the first formal dispatch ever sent through a telegraphic wire connecting remote places with each other: 'WHAT HATH GOD **WROUGHT**'.

'Workers of all lands, unite!'

By the mid-nineteenth century the new system of producing goods in large factories had taken hold in Great Britain, several other European countries and the United States. Political thinkers argued about whether the system – which created terrible poverty as well as great wealth – could be improved, or should be replaced. One of these thinkers, a German called Karl Marx, developed a set of political ideas known as **communism**.

Other political thinkers had proposed versions of **socialism**, which called for a fairer distribution of wealth. Marx took this idea much further. He argued that people tend to support the interests of their own **class**, and that the classes struggle against each other. By the 1840s the factory-owning class – which Marx called **bourgeois** – controlled money and power. It was only a matter of time, he continued, until the working class would overthrow the bourgeois class and seize power. This idea shook the world and led to several communist revolutions (notably in Russia and China) in the twentieth century. By the end of the twentieth century most countries had abandoned communism, although some are still ruled according to Marx's ideas today.

Modern Industry has converted the little workshop of the patriarchal master into the great factory of the industrial capitalist. Masses of labourers, crowded into the factory, are organized like soldiers. As privates of the industrial army, they are placed under the command of a perfect **hierarchy** of officers and sergeants. Not only are they slaves of the bourgeois class, and of the bourgeois state; they are daily and hourly enslaved by the machine, by the overlooker, and, above all, by the individual bourgeois manufacturer himself. The more openly this **despotism** proclaims gain to be its end and aim, the more petty, the more hateful and the more embittering it is.

Karl Marx's extreme ideas had a great influence around the world. His beliefs led to violent revolutions in some countries.

The arrival of oil

People had known about **crude oil** for thousands of years. Until the nineteenth century it was used mainly as a **lubricant**, a waterproofing aid and even as a medicine. Oil also burned slowly and might be useful as a fuel, but no one could find enough of it to replace whale oil as a household and industrial fuel. By the mid-1800s, however, English scientists had developed a method of **refining** crude oil to make it useful as a fuel. The question still remained of how to find enough crude oil to make this process work.

People had known for many decades that western Pennsylvania in the USA had supplies of crude oil, but before the mid nineteenth century it seemed impossible to extract it. One of the biggest problems seemed to be raising enough money to pay for drilling. One group of hopeful oil miners in the 1840s had gone to great lengths to build up interest in the oil in the area. They even faked a letter which they claimed was written by a French colonial soldier in the eighteenth century. In the letter, the soldier described a Native American fire-worshipping ceremony in which the oil-covered Allegheny River had burst into flames. The truth soon emerged that the letter was a fake, but many engineers continued to work on the problem of reaching the crude oil.

The solution came in Titusville, Pennsylvania, in 1859. An American engineer, Edwin Drake, developed a method of drilling for oil using an iron pipe – similar to the method used for drilling wells for water. Drake and other engineers had already noticed how oil had seeped into deep wells that had been dug for water and salt. He then considered using a similar method to drill for oil itself. Drake was well aware that western Pennsylvania was rich in oil, so he believed that an oil well would have a good chance there.

Drake used his invention, sinking a pipe 21 metres into the ground, and was able to draw out crude oil. The effect was staggering, and created an 'oil rush' that rivalled California's 'Gold Rush' of 1849. A new industry had been born.

A splendid thing is the Crossley well! A diamond of the first water! Enough of itself to silence the cry of humbug; to create a sensation of rival interests or inspire hope in many toiling for subterranean treasure, and to make every son of Pennsylvania rejoice in the good Providence that has enriched the state, not only with vast mines of iron and coal but also with rivers of oil!

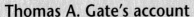

Wearing a top hat, American engineer Edwin Drake stands by the oil well he drilled. He was the first person to drill successfully for oil.

The power of the voice

By the 1870s huge networks of telegraph wires linked cities in the USA and in many European countries. The telegraph offered instant communications, but only in the form of dots and dashes picked up by telegraph receivers. Inventors set about trying to transmit and record sounds, especially the human voice. The first breakthrough came in 1876. A Scottish-born American inventor, Alexander Graham Bell, developed a machine (the telephone) that would pick up sounds and change them into electrical signals that could be transmitted down a line and then changed back to sounds at the other end.

The phonograph, a machine for recording and playing back sounds, was invented in the USA in 1877. Thomas Edison recorded sound on a cylinder which rotated against a needle, creating grooves. Playing the needle back against these grooves produced vibrations that were **amplified** to produce sounds. Edison and other inventors soon improved on this early phonograph, to develop machines that could clearly reproduce music and the human voice.

Alexander Graham Bell makes the first telephone call from New York to Chicago. He had invented the telephone sixteen years earlier, in 1876.

An extract from *Scribner's Monthly Magazine*

By the 1870s educated people were aware of – and interested
in – new developments in the field of science and **technology**.
This passage from *Scribner's Monthly Magazine* introduces a
detailed explanation of the telephone and the phonograph.

April 1878

The telephone and the phonograph.

Two recent American inventions are at the present
moment exciting the wonder and admiration of the
civilized world. The first, known as the telephone, or
far-speaker, is a device for transmitting to a
distance over an electric circuit, and accurately
reproducing thereat, all kinds of sounds, including
those of the human voice; the second, called by its
inventor the phonograph, or sound-recorder, is a
device for permanently recording and faithfully
reproducing, at any time or place, all kinds of
sounds, including those of the human voice.

The function of the telephone can be compared to that
of a speaking-tube capable of almost infinite
extension, through which conversation may be carried
on as readily as with persons in the same room. The
function of the phonograph is to stereotype the actual
tones of the human voice, so that they may be
preserved or bottled up, as it were, and kept for
future use.

Although a description of these inventions must
necessarily partake of somewhat more scientific
character than is usually found in the columns of a
popular magazine, I shall endeavor to make it as free
from technicalities possible.

Lighting the way

For thousands of years people depended on fire to provide light. Open flames, torches and candles relied on some sort of burning fuel to produce the light. By the early nineteenth century many cities piped gas into a series of street lamps to produce light. Gas lamps, however, created soot and they were also risky – a gas explosion could be very dangerous. Scientists began to explore ways of using electricity as a safer, cheaper method for lighting.

Experiments proved that electricity passing through a wire produces heat, and if the heat increases to a certain point the wire also produces light. However, the air surrounding the wire soon burnt it away. In 1879 American inventor Thomas Edison and British engineer Joseph Swan each developed a way of removing the air from a bulb that had a wire passing through it. An electrical current passing through that wire produced a bright light that continued to shine. Edison called his invention the **incandescent** lamp, and most modern light bulbs use the method he developed.

Thomas Edison, seen here in his New Jersey laboratory, was a tireless worker who recorded more than 1000 inventions before his death in 1931.

Thomas Edison explains his discovery

This passage is part of an article Edison wrote in 1880 for the *North American Review*. In it he explains the principles of his incandescent lamp, using scientific terms that he knew were by then familiar.

The perfected lamp consists of an oval bulb of glass about five inches in height, pointed at one end, and with a short stem three quarters of an inch in diameter at the other. Two wires of platinum enter the bulb through this stem, supporting the loop or f-shaped thread of carbon, which is about two inches in height. The stem is sealed after the introduction of the carbon loop. At its pointed end the bulb terminates in an open tube through which the air in the bulb is exhausted by means of a mercury-pump till not over one millionth part remains; the tube is then closed.

When the circuit is made, the resistance offered to the passage of the electric current by the carbon causes the loop to acquire a high temperature and to become incandescent; but, as this takes place in a vacuum, the carbon is not consumed. The life of a carbon loop through which a current is passed continuously varies from seven hundred and fifty to nine hundred hours.

The light is designed to serve precisely the same purposes in domestic use as gaslights. It requires no shade, no screen of ground glass, to modify its intensity, but can be gazed at without dazzling the eyes. The amount of light is equal to that given by the gas-jets in common use; but the light is steadier, and consequently less trying to the eyes. It is also a purer light than gas, being white, while gaslight is yellow.

The price of progress

Great Britain led the way in the Industrial Revolution and benefited from its advances – but it was also one of the first to feel its costs. **Reformers** and politicians had been aware of these costs from the time of the first factories, and some laws helped ease the conditions of working children (see pages 20–21). However, new problems developed. London and other British industrial cities became overcrowded, and many people lived in unhealthy conditions.

Overcrowding was a problem in itself, but it also led to serious health concerns. Poor **hygiene** and water supplies led to outbreaks of serious illnesses, which spread quickly through the crowded streets. Most of the victims of these diseases were poor working people. Coupled with disease was the problem of drunkenness: many working men spent their pay on drink. The **Temperance** Movement, as well as religious groups such as the Salvation Army, tried to combat the problems of alcohol. Writers also began to publicize terrible living and working conditions, both in Great Britain and in other industrial countries. Ida M. Tarbell and other crusading American journalists earned the nickname 'muckrakers' because of their efforts to expose these conditions. Their efforts were echoed in the works of French novelist Emile Zola and other writers.

Britain's new industrial wealth came at a cost. Workers lived in overcrowded, grimy conditions which often led to disease.

George Sims' experience

How the Poor Live (1889), by George Sims, was one of many accounts of living conditions in Britain's cities. In this passage, the author describes a visit to a family living in London.

I was the other day in a room occupied by a widow woman, her daughters of seventeen and sixteen, her sons of fourteen and thirteen, and two younger children. Her wretched apartment was on the street level, and behind it was a common yard of the **tenement**. For this room, the widow paid four and sixpence a week; the walls were mildewed and steaming with damp; the boards as you trod upon them made the slushing noise of a plant spread across a mud puddle in a brickfield.

Of all the evils arising from this one room system there is perhaps none greater than the utter destruction of innocence in the young. A moment's thought will enable the reader to appreciate the evils of it. But if it is bad in the case of a respectable family, how much more terrible is it when the children are familiarised with actual immorality.

It is by shutting our eyes to evils that we allow them to continue unreformed for so long. I maintain that such cases as these are fit ones for **legislative** protection. The **State** should have the power of rescuing its future citizens from such surroundings, and the law which protects young children from practical hurt should also be so framed as to protect them from moral destruction.

It is better that the ratepayers should bear a portion of the burden of new homes for the respectable poor than that they should have to pay twice as much in the long-run for prisons, lunatic asylums and workhouses.

Transatlantic signals

Understanding and using electrical energy lay behind many of the breakthroughs of the late nineteenth century. By the end of the century, telephone lines joined telegraph lines in huge networks running through many countries. Of course there was a major obstacle to all long-distance communications: the sea. A number of cables had been laid across the Atlantic Ocean, but these were expensive and could break.

The Italian scientist Guglielmo Marconi became fascinated by the notion of transmitting and receiving long-distance telegraph messages without the need for costly cables. Knowing that light and electricity are just part of **electromagnetic** radiation, he experimented on ways to send and receive radio waves. These radio waves would be used in the same way as Morse's telegraph used electrical signals – and there would be no need for wires. Marconi developed his method of 'wireless telegraphy' and in 1901 transmitted his first transatlantic radio message from Poldhu, Cornwall, to St John's, Newfoundland in North America.

Guglielmo Marconi raises the kite which carries part of his equipment. Here, on the coast of Newfoundland, the first transatlantic message was received.

Guglielmo Marconi's account

Marconi sat in a hut on the cliffs at St John's, Newfoundland, on 12 December 1901, waiting for the first transatlantic message. When it did arrive, the message consisted of just one letter, 'S', but it changed the world of communications for ever.

Shortly before mid-day I placed the single earphone to my ear and started listening. The receiver on the table before me was very crude – a few coils and **condensers** and a **coherer** – no valves, no amplifiers, not even a crystal. But I was at last on the point of putting the correctness of all my beliefs to the test. The answer came at 12.30 when I heard, faintly but distinctly, pip-pip-pip [**Morse code** for the letter 'S']. I handed the phone to Kemp: 'Can you hear anything?' I asked. 'Yes', he said, 'the letter S' – he could hear it. I knew then that all my anticipations had been justified. The electric waves sent out into space from Poldhu had crossed the Atlantic – the distance, enormous as it seemed then, of 1700 miles – unimpeded by the curvature of the earth. The result meant much more to me than mere successful realization of my experiment. As Sir Oliver Lodge has stated, it was an **epoch** in history. I now felt for the first time absolutely certain that the day would come when mankind would be able to send messages without wires not only across the Atlantic but between the farthermost ends of the earth.

Into the air

'The sky's the limit' was the claim of inventors at the start of the twentieth century, but to some people that was too confining. Air travel, in a powered aircraft, was a goal for many engineers. Hot-air balloons had been travelling for more than a century, sometimes thousands of metres in the air, but they depended on the wind to go anywhere.

Around 1900 two American bicycle mechanics, Orville and Wilbur Wright, began developing a practical powered aircraft. They studied the flight of birds and observed the path of gliders to help their designing. They also knew that they could use a recent invention, the **internal combustion engine**, to power such an aircraft.

By 1903 their first aeroplane, the *Flyer*, was ready and they took it to a beach in North Carolina to test it. The brothers tossed a coin to see who would make the first flight. Wilbur won, but the test failed because of high winds. Orville's successful flight, on 17 December 1903, became the first step in the field of aviation.

Orville Wright's first flight in 1903 lasted only 12 seconds, but it was the beginning of today's huge air industry. Wilbur Wright runs alongside his brother.

The course of the flight up and down was exceedingly erratic, partly due to the irregularity of the air, and partly to lack of experience in handling this machine. The control of the front rudder was difficult on account of its being balanced too near the center. This gave it a tendency to turn itself when started; so that it turned too far on one side and then too far on the other. As a result the machine would rise suddenly to about ten feet, and then as suddenly dart for the ground. A sudden dart when a little over a hundred feet from the end of the track, or a little over 120 feet from the point at which it rose into the air, ended the flight. As the velocity of the wind was over 35 feet per second and the speed of the machine over the ground against this wind ten feet per second, the speed of the machine relative to the air was over 45 feet per second, and the length of the flight was equivalent to a flight of 540 feet made in calm air.

This flight lasted only 12 seconds, but it was nevertheless the first in the history of the world in which a machine carrying a man had raised itself by its own power into the air in full flight, had sailed forward without reduction of speed and had finally landed at a point as high as that from which it started.

The assembly line

The American industrialist Henry Ford was not the first person to produce an automobile – the new invention was nearly 20 years old when he founded the Ford Motor Company in 1903. However, Ford did introduce something very dramatic: from 1908 he produced his Model T cars on an **assembly line** with interchangeable parts. This method reduced the cost and increased the speed of production, making cars affordable for ordinary people.

Ford is also remembered for another reason. He understood that work on an assembly line was boring and that many workers would want to leave. He also knew that constantly hiring and training new workers was expensive, so Ford began offering his workers better-than-average pay to keep them in the company. That experiment proved to be a success, and in 1926 he took it a stage further. This time he reduced the working week from six days to five but paid workers a full week's wage. It was partly an act of kindness, but it made good business sense too. If people had good pay and more time off, they would be able to spend their money on a range of products – including Ford cars.

Assembly lines in Henry Ford's factories increased speed and efficiency. Cars could now be produced cheaply, so ordinary people could afford to buy them.

An interview with Henry Ford

This passage comes from a 1926 interview with Henry Ford in the magazine *World's Work*. In it Ford explains the reasons why he reduced the working week for his staff.

The country is ready for the five day week. It is bound to come through all industry. In adopting it ourselves, we are putting it into effect in about fifty industries, for we are coal miners, iron miners, lumbermen, and so on. The short week is bound to come, because without it the country will not be able to absorb its production and stay prosperous.

The harder we crowd business for time, the more efficient it becomes. The more well-paid leisure workmen get, the greater become their wants. These wants soon become needs. Well-managed business pays high wages and sells at low prices. Its workmen have the leisure to enjoy life and the wherewithal with which to finance that enjoyment.

The industry of this country could not long exist if factories generally went back to the ten hour day, because the people would not have the time to consume the goods produced. For instance, a workman would have little use for an automobile if he had to be in the shops from dawn until dusk. And that would react in countless directions, for the automobile, by enabling people to get about quickly and easily, gives them a chance to find out what is going on in the world – which leads them to a larger life that requires more food, more and better goods, more books, more music – more of everything. The benefits of travel are not confined to those who can take an expensive foreign trip. There is more to learn in this country than there is abroad.

What have we learnt from the Industrial Revolution?

People in the twenty-first century have grown used to seeing new products and technological advances. We are no different from people in the 1880s as they saw telephones, phonographs and electric lights for the first time, but we have also seen many of the side-effects of the Industrial Revolution. We know that the oil will one day run out, and that we are polluting our water and atmosphere. Overcrowding, poor health conditions and poverty remain problems. We have come to understand that 'development' – the path from a farming way of life to an industrial one – comes with many costs. We are beginning to realize that these costs affect the whole world.

By looking back at the history of the Industrial Revolution we can share in the excitement as people saw the world around them transformed. We can also remember that, right from the start, there were voices calling for caution and care along the way. These voices continue to remind us of our global responsibility.

At the end of the nineteenth century people's lives were transformed as countries developed from farming communities into industrial nations.

Akiko Domoto's view
This passage is part of an article written by Akiko Domoto, a
senior Japanese politician, for the United Nations in 1999. In it
she looks ahead at the ways in which development and scientific
advances can continue the spirit of the Industrial Revolution,
while lessening its cost to society.

The occurrence of what we now refer to as the
'industrial revolution' was unprecedented in human
history. With the **compartmentalization** and
specialization of knowledge came exciting scientific
discoveries and rapid technological advancements. The
development of the steam and **internal combustion
engines**, and the discovery of bacteria and viruses,
led to extraordinary improvements in the well-being
of a significant proportion of the world's
population.

From the very start, the rise of modern industry and
science had its dark side, but the true extent of
that dark side did not become evident until the
latter half of this century. Localized pollution and
the disappearance of animal **habitat** in the late
eighteenth century have given way to environmental
problems on a global scale: the thinning of the ozone
layer; depletion of fish stocks; the pervasive
presence of persistent organic pollutants in human
and animal populations; the loss of **biodiversity**; and
the rapid shifts in the earth's climate. While
localized environmental problems can, to an extent,
be solved by **legislation** and **technology**, problems
that are planetary in scale require a sweeping shift
in the way we legislate, govern, produce and learn.

Timeline

1705	Thomas Newcomen builds the first successful steam engine
1709	Abraham Darby uses **coke** to **smelt** iron ore
1761	Bridgewater Canal completed
1764	James Hargreaves invents the spinning jenny, which paves the way for a mechanized **textile** industry
1775	James Watt's first efficient steam engine
1785	Edmund Cartwright patents the power loom
1789	Thames-Severn Canal links the Thames to the Bristol Channel
1792	William Murdock lights his home with coal gas
1793	Eli Whitney develops his cotton gin (a device to remove the seeds from raw cotton)
1801	Robert Trevithick runs a steam locomotive (called 'Catch me who can') in London
1807	Robert Fulton's *Clermont* is the first successful steamboat
1811–15	Luddite riots: labourers attack factories and break up the machines they fear will replace them
1821	Charles Babbage develops his Difference Engine –the forerunner of the computer
1825	The Stockton to Darlington (England) service becomes the first public railway
1825–43	Isambard Kingdom Brunel builds the first underwater tunnel, under the Thames
1830	Manchester & Liverpool Railway begins first regular commercial rail service
1831	Michael Faraday discovers **electromagnetic** current, making possible generators and electric engines
1834	William Fox Talbot produces photographs
1837	Samuel F. B. Morse develops the telegraph and **Morse Code**
1843	SS *Great Britain* – first large, iron, screw-propelled steamship
1844	Commercial use of Morse's telegraph (Baltimore to Washington)
1850	Oil **refining** first used
1851	Isaac Singer invents first practical sewing machine
1855	First skyscraper (ten stories) built in Chicago
1859	Edwin Drake strikes oil in Pennsylvania
1873	James Clerk Maxwell states the laws of **electromagnetic radiation**
1876	Alexander Graham Bell invents the telephone
1877	Thomas Edison invents the phonograph
1879	Thomas Edison invents the **incandescent** lamp
1885	Karl Benz develops first automobile to run on an **internal combustion engine**
1900	First powered balloon built
1901	Marconi receives first transatlantic radio message
1903	Wright brothers make first powered flight
1908	Henry Ford mass-produces the Model T car

Find out more

Books and websites

Turning Points: The Steam Engine, Richard Tames, (Heinemann Library, 1999)
Living through History: Britain 1750–1900 N. Kelly, R. Rees, J. Shuter
(Heinemann, 1999)
History of Britain: Victorian Britain, Andrew Langley (Hamlyn, 1994)

Go exploring! Log on to Heinemann's online history resource at
www.heinemannexplore.co.uk

You can also use the keywords: 'Industrial Revolution'; 'primary source': 'document'
to lead you into dozens of fascinating websites. These two will get you started:

www.historyteacher.net/APEuroCourse/APEuro_Main_Weblinks_Page.htm
This site has a variety of primary sources and several sound files for downloading

www.fordham.edu/halsall/mod/modsbook14.html and ... 35.html
Primary sources from the Industrial Revolution, and links to other events in the
eighteenth and nineteenth centuries

List of primary sources

The author and publisher gratefully acknowledge the following publications and
websites from which written sources in the book are drawn. In some cases the
wording or sentence structure has been simplified to make the material more
appropriate for a school readership

P 9: Benjamin Franklin: *Autobiography of Benjamin*, ed John Bigelow (Philadelphia, J. B. Lippincott and
Company, 1868), from website: http://www.cc.ukans.edu/carrie/docs/texts/franklin_how_note.html
P 11: Daniel Defoe: *The Faber Book of Reportage*, ed John Carey. (Faber & Faber, 1987)
P 13: Thomas Jefferson: *The Works of Thomas Jefferson in Twelve Volumes*, collected and edited by
Paul Leicester Ford. Federal Edition
P 15: '*Observations on the Loss of Woollen Spinning*':http://www.fordham.edu/halsall/mod/1794woolens.html
P 17: Peter Smart: http://history.hanover.edu/courses/excerpts/111sad.html
P 19: Archibald Prentice: http://www.spartacus.schoolnet.co.uk/PRperceval.htm
P 21: newspaper article: www.dmm.org.uk/names/n1821-01.htm
P 23: Charles Babbage: home.clara.net/mycetes/babbage/Babjourn.htm
P 25: Canal mania: *The Faber Book of Reportage*, ed John Carey (Faber & Faber, 1987).
P 27: Robert Fulton: http://www.history.rochester.edu/steam/thurston/fulton/chapter6.htm
P 29: Peter Cooper: http://www.railroadextra.com/abrw15.html
P 31: Fox Talbot: www.rleggat.com/photohistory/history/talbot.htm
P 33: Article: *Harper's Magazine* (1844)
P 35: Karl Marx: *Communist Manifesto*, Karl Marx and Friedrich Engels, Penguin Classics (Penguin, 2002)
P 37: Thomas A Gate: 1.www.scripophily.net/oilcreekanda.html 2. www.allegheny-
online.com/venangohist.html
P 39: *Scribner's Monthly magazine* (April 1878), the article entitled *The telephone and the phonograph*.
P 41: Thomas Edison: *North American Review* (1880)
P 43: George Sims: www.spartacus.schoolnet.co.uk/ITlondon.htm
P 45: Guglielmo Marconi: *The Faber Book of Reportage*, ed John Carey (Faber & Faber, 1987).
P 47: Orville Wright: sln.fi.edu/flights/first/during.html
P 49: Henry Ford: www.vcn.bc.ca/timework/ford.htm
P 51: Akiko Domoto: www.un.org/Pubs/chronicle/1999/issue2/0299p72.htm

Glossary

amplified   made stronger or louder

aqueduct   bridge that carries water across a valley

assembly line   method of producing goods in which each worker concentrates on a single part

bias   existing opinion about someone or something that makes it hard to be fair

biodiversity   overall range of animal and plant life

bobbin   wooden or metal tube around which thread is wound

bound   owned by an employer or sold to an employer

bourgeois   term (often insulting) for the class that owns factories and shops

camera lucida   instrument attached to the eyepiece of a microscope that projects the image on to a sheet where it can be traced

camera obscura   darkened box with an opening and a lens which projects an image on to a flat surface

charcoal   fuel that is produced by heating wood with little oxygen so that it will not burn away

class   group of people who share a similar way of earning a living

coherer   device used to collect radio waves

coke   burnable fuel that is left when coal is refined

colliery   coal mine

communism   political system or way of thinking that calls for the government to own all property and to provide work for the people

compartmentalization   dividing people and things into many separate categories

condenser   device for collecting and holding an electric charge

crude oil   oil as it is found in its natural state, before refining

deforestation   cutting down trees and not replacing them

despotism   government based on the brutal use of power

documentary   providing accurate information

durable   long-lasting

economy   overall system of work, payment, business etc within a country

electromagnetic radiation   the process by which energy is radiated (sent out) by waves and tiny particles; the size of the wave corresponds to a different type of radiation (radio waves, visible light, X-rays and so on)

emolument   payment for a service

epoch   particular time that is noted for a single dramatic event

export   send goods to another country for sale, or one of those goods

folly   foolish project

habitat   natural living area of a plant or animal

hierarchy   system of persons ranked one above the other

hygiene   cleanliness (especially as a means of avoiding disease)

inaugural   marking the first occasion of something

incandescent   producing light by being heated

inflammable   able to burn easily

internal combustion engine   engine powered by the gases formed by burning fuel

joiner   someone whose job is to make things out of wood

legislate   to bring into law

legislation   passage of laws by a government

lubricant   something (usually a liquid) that reduces friction and helps things to move more easily

mania   crazy concentration on a particular idea

manifesto   written statement of beliefs

Morse code series of dots and dashes corresponding to letters and numbers produced by starting and stopping an electrical current in a telegraph message

ore rock that contains metal

patriarchal having a father-like power over other people

primary source original record describing a historical event or era

processing working on an ore or other natural ingredient to separate the elements that make it up

raw material basic materials needed to produce goods

redresser someone who intends to set right a wrong

refining type of processing that removes materials that are not wanted

reformer someone who wants to improve conditions, usually for the poor

revolutionaries people who believe that society can only be changed through a revolution, dramatically replacing an old way of life with something new

sabotage deliberate destruction of something by some hidden method

secondary source historical record that is written by someone who was not present when an event took place

share part ownership in a company which individuals can buy

smelter furnace used to heat and melt ore in order to separate and remove the metal

socialism theory or system of government that calls for public ownership of many businesses in order to look after everyone in society

speculator someone who buys shares as a way of gambling on gaining money and with little interest in the company

state another word for a country's government

subscribe putting one's name down on a list to show interest in buying shares in a particular company

technology use of science for industrial purposes

temperance not using alcohol, and persuading others not to do so

tenement overcrowded block of flats

textile any cloth or goods produced by weaving or knitting

turner someone who makes pots

unapprenticed not trained to take on a job in the traditional manner (which called for many years of training but guaranteed someone a job at the end)

vacuum enclosed space from which all air has been extracted

warp set of yarns placed lengthways in a loom; the crossways threads are called the weft

wrought worked or made

Some of the sources use imperial measurements; here is a chart to help you convert them to metric. ⇩

To convert:	
Inches to centimetres:	multiply by 2.5400
Feet to metres:	multiply by 0.3048
Yards to metres:	multiply by 0.9144
Miles to kilometres:	multiply by 1.6090

In the old currency a pound (£) was divided into 20 shillings (s.). Each shilling contained 12 pence (d.).

Index